live it *learn it*

BIBLE STUDIES

FRUIT OF THE SPIRIT

Group
Loveland, Colorado

Group's R.E.A.L. Guarantee to you:

This Group resource incorporates our R.E.A.L. approach to ministry—one that encourages long-term retention and life transformation. It's ministry that's:

Relational

Because learner-to-learner interaction enhances learning and builds Christian friendships.

Experiential

Because what learners experience through discussion and action sticks with them up to 9 times longer than what they simply hear or read.

Applicable

Because the aim of Christian education is to equip learners to be both hearers and doers of God's Word.

Learner-based

Because learners understand and retain more when the learning process takes into consideration how they learn best.

Learn It, Live It Bible Studies™: Fruit of the Spirit

Copyright © 2003 Group Publishing, Inc.

Visit our Web site: **www.grouppublishing.com**

Credits

Contributors: Joe Beckler, Keith Madsen, K.C. Mason, and G. Brenton Mock
Editor: Beth Rowland
Development Editor: Matt Lockhart
Chief Creative Officer: Joani Schultz
Copy Editor: Loma Huh
Art Director: Randy Kady
Print Production Artist: Susan Tripp
Cover Art Director: Jeff A. Storm
Cover Designer: Toolbox Creative
Cover Photographer: Daniel Treat
Production Manager: Dodie Tipton

ISBN 0-7644-2669-9
10 9 8 7 6 5 4 3 2 1   12 11 10 09 08 07 06 05 04 03

Printed in the United States of America.

Contents

Introduction to Group's
Learn It, Live It Bible Studies™

Welcome to an exciting new concept in small-group Bible studies! At Group, we recognize the value of Bible study to Christian growth—there's no better way to grow in our faith than to study the living Word of God. We also know the value of group activity. Activity helps us practice what we learn. And this is vital to the Christian faith: Jesus doesn't tell us simply to learn about him—he asks us to become like him in thoughts, in words, and in actions. That's why Group developed *Learn It, Live It Bible Studies*™. In these studies you'll be challenged to not only learn more about God but to put what you've learned into practice in a powerful and meaningful way.

Whether you're new to Bible study or a seasoned pro, you'll find each lesson's Bible study to be interesting and compelling. You'll open God's Word with the others in your group. You'll study relevant Scripture passages and discuss thought-provoking questions that will help you all grow in your faith and in your understanding of who God is and what he wants for your life.

After the Bible study, you'll be invited to choose a group project that will help you practice the very thing you've just learned. Some of these projects are simple, easy, and low-risk. Others will require a greater commitment of time and resources—they may even take you beyond your comfort zone. But whichever group project you choose to do, you can be certain that it will help you grow more like Christ in your everyday life.

We hope you enjoy these lessons! And we pray that by studying these lessons and doing these projects, you'll find yourself becoming more and more like our Lord Jesus Christ.

Fruit of the Spirit

This nine-session Bible study focuses on Galatians 5:22-23, the fruit of the Spirit. The Christians in Galatia were confused about their faith. Error had crept into their teaching, and the church was becoming more and more legalistic. Paul wrote to the Galatians to call them back to the gospel of grace. Paul explained in very strong language that everything we are, as Christians, comes from God and from Christ's death and resurrection. There is nothing to gain by keeping the Jewish law—our salvation comes solely from our faith in Christ.

Paul passionately urged the Galatians to live a life of freedom in the Holy Spirit rather than to fall back into the pointless practice of living by the law. He eloquently compared the life the Galatians had left, a life controlled by the sinful nature, to the life they can have in Christ, a life guided by God's Holy Spirit. Living by the sinful nature is a life of slavery and it produces wickedness. Living by the Spirit produces the fruit of the Spirit: love, joy, peace, patience, kindness, goodness, faithfulness, gentleness, and self-control. This Bible study will help you learn about each of these qualities and how you can live by God's Spirit and grow in fruitfulness.

About the Sessions

Start It *(15 minutes)*

This part of the lesson is designed to introduce everyone to the day's topic and to get your discussion flowing. Here you'll find an introduction to read over and a quick warm-up to do together, along with a few discussion questions.

Study It *(45-60 minutes)*

This is the Bible study portion of the lesson. Every lesson provides several Scripture passages to look up and 9 to 12 discussion questions for you to talk over as a group. Feel free to jot down your insights in the space provided.

You'll also notice that each lesson includes extra information in the margins. You'll find Bible facts, definitions, and quotations. Please note that the information doesn't always come from a Christian perspective. These margin notes are meant to be thought-provoking and to get your group discussing each topic at a deeper level.

Close It *(15-30 minutes)*

During the Close It section of the lesson, you'll do two things. First, you'll read through the Live It options at the end of the lesson and choose one to do together as a group. You'll find more information about the Live It options in the next section.

Second, you'll pray together as a group. Be sure to take the time to listen to each other's prayer requests. You may want to write those prayer requests in the space provided so you can pray for those requests throughout the week. Don't rush your time with God. Praying with others is a precious opportunity— make the most of it!

Part 2: **live it**

In each lesson in this study, you'll find five Live It options. These group activities are designed to help your Bible study group live out what you learned in the Bible study. Together as a group, read over the Live It options each week. Then choose one to do together. You'll find that some of the activities are quick and easy and can be done without planning an extra session. Other activities will require more time and planning. Some activities are very low-risk. Others might push group members to the edge of their comfort zone. Some of the activities are suitable for entire families to participate in. Others will work better if you arrange for child care. Choose the option that interests your group the most and carry it out. You'll find that you learn much more when you practice it in real life.

Love

Love—the Beatles told us it was *all* we need. We might debate whether that is literally true, but there can be little doubt that love is what many, if not most, yearn for. In our quest for love, we need to remember an old saying: "Love isn't love until you give it away." To find love, we have to learn to love.

That's why it's significant that love is the first quality of the fruit of the Spirit Paul mentions. When we have the Holy Spirit in our lives, the Spirit helps us love others. The Spirit does that by planting and growing the love of Jesus Christ within us. We are told in 1 John 4:19, "We love because he first loved us."

It is not always easy to love others. We get impatient with our families. We're tempted to treat people at work as mere objects to use on our way toward our professional or financial goals. When we meet difficult people, we often want to strike out at them, or at least get away from them. However, when we cannot love through our own power, we can do so by the Spirit. When we have the Spirit in our lives, we can be confident that the Spirit will help us to love in these difficult situations.

This lesson will help you see what it means to rely on the Spirit to help you love the people around you. Through what you read and hear from others, as well as through what you do individually and with others, you'll learn to give the love that you also want to receive.

Part 1: *learn it*

Start It *(15 minutes)*

Love Talk

To get started with today's lesson, choose one or two of the following questions to answer with your group:

- **If you were to publish your own personal dictionary, whose picture would you put next to the definition of *love*?**

- **Finish this sentence: "If a person really loves me, he or she will..."**

- **If you were to talk to a group of children about love, what one thing would you tell them that you have learned about love since you were their age?**

> "Tony Campolo sometimes asks students at secular universities what they know about Jesus. Can they recall anything that Jesus said? By clear consensus they reply, 'Love your enemies.' More than any other teaching of Christ, that one stands out to an unbeliever. Such an attitude is unnatural, perhaps downright suicidal. It's hard enough to forgive your rotten brothers, as Joseph did, but your enemies? The gang of thugs down the block? Iraqis? The drug dealers poisoning our nation?"
>
> **Philip Yancey,**
> ***What's So Amazing About Grace?***

Study It *(45-60 minutes)*

> If you have a large group, form smaller groups of four to seven people to answer the discussion questions. At the end of the Study It section, allow time for the subgroups to report to the whole group.

Read the quotation from Philip Yancey.

1. Why do you think students at secular universities remember that Jesus taught about love? What role does love have in the world?

Read John 13:34-35.

    2. Why is it important for Christians to be loving? List as many reasons as you can think of.

    3. Is it possible to be a Christian without being loving? Explain.

In groups of two or three, select one or two of the following passages:

- *Matthew 5:43-48*
- *Luke 10:25-37*
- *John 15:9-13*
- *I Corinthians 13:1-13*
- *I John 4:7-12, 16b-20*

    4. In your group, read and discuss your verses. What is the most important insight this passage gives you about love? What is the biggest challenge that this passage presents for you? After a few minutes, each group should give a summary of their passage to the whole group and report their insights.

Meanings of Love

There are four Greek words that mean "love":

Eros: This means romantic or sexual love. It is love based on the natural biological attraction that is at the basis of reproduction.

Phileo: This means what we commonly call "brotherly love." It is love based on common interests and the affinity one might have for someone who has a similar view of life.

Stergo: This means the love between parents and children. It can sometimes refer to the love between a pet and its owner or the love a people feel for their ruler.

Agape: This means love without expectation of receiving a benefit in return. It is the kind of love that God has for us. This is the word that Paul uses in Galatians 5:22 when he says the fruit of the Spirit is "love."

5. What happens when we, as Christians, live lives of love? What makes living a life of love difficult?

6. When a Christian has a difficult time loving a person or a group of people, what can he or she do?

Read the margin note about the different definitions of love.

7. When people think of the word *love*, what do they usually mean?

8. What does it mean to you that the kind of love Paul says is the fruit of the Spirit is *agape*? What do you need to do to start showing this fruit more in your life?

9. How does the Holy Spirit grow the fruit of love in our lives? What is our role in becoming people who are known for loving others?

Read the quotation from Anne Lamott. Also read Proverbs 17:17.

10. How have friends shown you this kind of love? What happens to relationships when people show God's love to each other?

> "This is the most profound spiritual truth I know: that even when we're most sure that love can't conquer all, it seems to anyway. It goes down into the rat hole with us, in the guise of our friends, and there it swells and comforts."
>
> **Anne Lamott, *Traveling Mercies: Some Thoughts on Faith***

Read Romans 5:6-8.

11. How did Jesus exemplify this idea of love going "down into the rat hole with us"?

Reread John 13:35.

12. If you made John 13:35 your personal mission statement, how would that affect your daily life? To answer this question, consider your career, your finances, your hobbies, your church life, your relationship with your family and neighbors, and all other components of your life.

Close It *(15-30 minutes)*

Review the options in the Live It section of this session and make plans as a group to complete one of these activities prior to moving on to the next session. This is your opportunity to move from theory to practice—*carpe diem!*

Pray It

Share prayer requests and close in prayer. Be sure to ask God to guide your efforts as you plan and carry out a Live It activity.

Plan It

What activity are we going to do?

When are we doing this?

Where will this take place?

Other: special instructions/my responsibility

Option 1

Plan a simple get-together after your church's next worship service. Have each person or family from your Bible study group invite a person or family from your church that none of you knows well. It would be great to invite people who are new to your church or people who don't appear to be well connected to your church's activities. Serve simple food such as sandwiches, chips, and cookies. Make it the priority of the get-together to get to know your guests and make them feel welcomed and loved.

Option 2

Throw a Valentine's party, regardless of what time of year it is. Decorate with red and pink hearts. Serve foods such as heart-shaped pizza, red soda pop, and heart-shaped cookies with pink icing. Before you eat, have each person pray for the person to their right, thanking God for one lovable thing about that person. Have each person bring a small gift (suitable for either gender) that will remind the recipient of God's love. For example, some-one might bring a small globe to help the recipient remember that God loves the entire world. After the meal, have the person with the birthday nearest February 14 choose a gift and open it. If it's not immediately apparent, have the giver explain how the gift relates to God's love. Then have the person whose birthday is next closest to February 14 choose the next gift, and so on until everyone has opened a gift.

When all the gifts have been opened, have each person think of someone outside of your group to whom he or she can pass on the gift received here, so that your small group can spread God's love to others. End the party with a time of prayer, thanking God for his love and asking God to help you show love to others.

Option 3

Individually, reach out to someone with whom you've had diffi-culty in the past. Perhaps it's someone you've had a disagreement with or someone who's been unkind to you. Choose one of the following ways to reach out to that person this week.

• Ask God to give you love for the person. Send a warm note to him or her, asking for forgiveness for your part in the conflict.

• Call the person on the phone or take him or her out for a cup of coffee or a soft drink. Express your appreciation for him or her. Seek to understand his or her point of view.

• Invite the person and his or her family over for dinner. Work to understand the person and make friends with him or her.

Afterwards, get together with your small group and have everyone share how their friendship overtures went. How did your "enemy" react to your demonstration of sincere Christian love? Talk about how it feels to love your enemies.

Option 4

There are many people who may feel lonely or love-deprived—for example, children who have a parent in prison. Log on to www.angeltree.org and find out about Prison Fellowship Ministries' work with children who have a parent in prison. Many are familiar with Angel Tree's Christmas ministry, but there are volunteer opportunities available year-round. Contact your local representative to find out what volunteer opportunities are available for your group to show God's love to these children.

Option 5

As a group, show love to a group the church tends to define as an enemy—those who work at or seek the services of an abortion clinic. Before you make any plans, pray together for the clinic where you've chosen to show love. Ask God to give you a tender and profound love for these people. Then choose a way you can show love to them this week.

Be careful to act in a way that won't condemn those who work there or those who go there for an abortion. Also be careful that your actions don't condone the decision these people have made. Choose an activity that will simply express that God loves the women who come to the clinic and those who work at the clinic. You may want to ask the clinic for permission to hand out small bouquets of flowers to the women one day.

Approach the clinic in the spirit of God's love. For example, you might say, "We know there has been plenty of ill will between Christians and those who seek the services of abortion clinics. That saddens us, because the truth of Christianity is that God loves all people. Would you allow us to reach out in love to the women who come to your clinic? We won't use this occasion for any kind of political positioning; we simply want to show love and respect to these women by giving them each a small bouquet of flowers."

Purchase several small bouquets. You may want to attach a card with John 3:16-17 on it or a simple message of God's deep love for people. Then, be respectful, kind, friendly, and loving as you hand out the flowers as people make their way into the clinic.

Debrief It

After experiencing this session's Live It activity, discuss these questions as a group:

- **On a scale of 1 (low) to 10 (high), how would you rank this experience for yourself? Why?**

- **What was the most important insight you gained from this experience?**

- **How can you incorporate this quality into your life regularly?**

Journal It

The following space is provided for you to record your personal thoughts, reflections, impressions or feelings about this session's topic and Live It activity.

Joy

Jesus said in John 10:10, "I have come that they may have life, and that they may have it more abundantly" (NKJV). To have life abundantly is more than to have a life that never ends; rather, it is to have life as God originally intended it to be, full of meaning and joy. But the truth is that many of us don't experience life in that way. For far too many of us, life too easily becomes humdrum.

Perhaps this is why writer C.S. Lewis titled the biography of his early life *Surprised by Joy*. He went from nominal Christianity to embracing atheism before finally being converted to a more vital Christian faith. Joy came to him after he despaired of ever finding it, and it came through a personal relationship with Jesus Christ.

Joy is something different than being happy or excited all of the time. No one is excited and happy *all* the time. Instead, joy is being able to maintain a strongly positive feeling about life and to praise God for life *even in the midst of sorrows and setbacks*. This is the quality Paul had and urged on others when he wrote from a Roman jail, "Rejoice in the Lord always. I will say it again: Rejoice!" (Philippians 4:4).

The Holy Spirit helps us to have and maintain this attitude of joy. In this study you will gain a greater understanding of what joy is and how you can have the fruit of joy in your life.

Part 1: learn it

Start It *(15 minutes)*

Sharing Celebrations

Share one sentence with the group about something that happened this past week that you'd like to celebrate. After everyone has shared, the group should celebrate in some way. It could be by singing the Doxology, or by reciting in unison one of the following Scripture passages: Psalm 103:1-2; Psalm 105:1; or Psalm 106:1.

Then choose one or two of the following questions to answer and share with the group:

- **What is the most joyful moment you can remember from your childhood?**

- **Which of the following is most likely to bring joy to your life as an adult: being around children? being outside on a beautiful day? being recognized for an accomplishment? spending time with loved ones or friends? something else?**

- **From your experiences, how would you define** *joy?* **How is it different from similar concepts, such as** *happiness, excitement,* **or** *ecstasy?*

Study It *(45-60 minutes)*

> If you have a large group, form smaller groups of four to seven people to answer the discussion questions. At the end of the Study It section, allow time for the subgroups to report to the whole group.

1. What do you think Buechner means by "the ultimate goodness and joy of things"?

> "...if you ever took truly to heart the ultimate goodness and joy of things, even at their bleakest, the need to praise someone or something for it would be so great that you might even have to go out and speak of it to the birds of the air."
>
> **Frederick Buechner,** *The Sacred Journey*

2. Do you agree that there is a goodness in life that seems to demand a response of praise? Why or why not? When have you felt such a strong sense of joy that you felt like shouting to whoever would listen?

3. Choose one or two of the following Scripture references. If your group is larger than ten people, form groups of two or three and divide the references among the groups. For each reference chosen, do the following: Identify the joyful person; discuss why the person is joyful; share whatever similar experiences you have had; and identify what the passage teaches you about joy. Then report your answers to the group.

- 2 Samuel 6:12-19
- Psalm 30
- Luke 2:8-20
- Luke 24:36-53
- Acts 2:42-47
- Philippians 1:18-26
- 1 Peter 1:3-9

4. How do you know when a person has great joy? Share a story about a joyful person you know.

5. When compared to the general population, would you say Christians tend to be more joyful? Explain.

Read 1 Peter 1:3-9.

6. What do Christians have to be joyful about? What does our joyfulness accomplish within the fellowship of Christians and also as a witness to the world?

"As I sat in an armchair watching my little daughter dance and my wife's face sparkle with life and joy, a wave of emotion like one of the waves of the ocean a few feet away from us washed over me, and I started to cry. I cried quietly, but Jeanne turned her face and saw me. The smile left her face but then it quickly returned...because she knew that at that moment I was happy. She knew I was crying not only out of sorrow but also out of joy, and that the joy was so powerful that it hurt. My joy was that I was there, on that beach under those stars listening to that music and watching the two people I loved more than anyone or anything in the world, and I did not want that feeling of perfect joy ever to end."

Arthur Ashe, while dying of AIDS, *Days of Grace*

Read the quotation from Arthur Ashe. Arthur died of AIDS shortly after writing this.

7. What is the connection between experiencing joy and having had the experience of pain? Why is this particularly relevant to the Christian life?

Read Matthew 5:11-12 and James 1:2-4.

8. How can we have joy in the midst of trial and pain?

9. How does the Holy Spirit bring about the fruit of joy in our lives?

10. What does a joyful life look like on an everyday basis? What would your life look like if you had the kind of joy Scripture calls us to?

Close It *(15-30 minutes)*

Review the options in the Live It section of this session and make plans as a group to complete one of these activities prior to moving on to the next session. This is your opportunity to move from theory to practice—*carpe diem!*

Pray It

Share prayer requests and close in prayer. Be sure to ask God to guide your efforts as you plan and carry out a Live It activity.

Plan It

What activity are we going to do?

When are we doing this?

Where will this take place?

Other: special instructions/my responsibility

Option 1

As a group, plan a celebration of joy—in other words, a party! Have each person or family bring and share these things:
- favorite joyful party food
- favorite joyful praise music
- at least five favorite clean jokes, funny stories, or cartoons that caused belly laughs

Option 2

Have each class member keep a "Journal of Joy" for the week. Each day have them write down at least two experiences that brought them joy. It could be a phone call from a friend, a moment they stopped and enjoyed their flower garden, a special time with a friend, a new insight from Scripture, or any experience that lifted them up. At the end of the week, have them share their journals with at least one other member of the class. If they choose, they might also want to share their journals with family members.

Option 3

Plan a joyful song night. Invite a guitar player or pianist from your church to lead your group in singing hymns, choruses, and other praise songs—whatever joyful music your group likes best. If you don't know a guitar player or pianist, have everyone bring in their favorite CDs and sing along with them. If your church has a CCLI license, you can type up lyrics sheets for the group.

Option 4

The phrase "shout for joy" is listed more than twenty times in the Bible. Plan a time together to read joyful psalms aloud and make a joyful noise unto the Lord. Have each person in the group bring copies of their favorite joyful psalm and enough joyful noisemakers for everyone in the group. Have each person type up their favorite psalm (making copies for everyone in the group) and indicate how the group will read the psalm aloud. For example, you might have half the men and half the women read aloud alternate verses to each other from across the room while the rest of the group plays "Awesome God" on kazoos. Someone else might choose to have everyone read aloud a psalm in an Irish accent. Have fun proclaiming the psalms joyfully with each other and celebrate the joy of knowing God.

Option 5

Plan an evening together to tell joyful stories about God. People may want to tell stories about when they've particularly enjoyed spending time with God. Some may share memories of what God has done for them or taught them. Others may share their hopes for what God will do in the future. And some may share Bible verses or passages that bring them joy. End your time together with prayer, praising God for the joy he's brought to you all.

Debrief It

After experiencing this session's Live It activity, discuss these questions as a group:

- **On a scale of 1 (low) to 10 (high), how would you rank this experience for yourself? Why?**

- **What was the most important insight you gained from this experience?**

- **How can you incorporate this quality into your life regularly?**

Journal It

The following space is provided for you to record your personal thoughts, reflections, impressions, or feelings about this session's topic and Live It activity.

Peace

We live in an age that is wrapped up in anxiety. We worry about terrorism; we worry about violence in our children's schools; we worry about global warming and ecological disaster; we worry about stock market plunges and rising jobless rates; and we worry about cancer and AIDS. In the midst of all these anxieties, what do we do? We work fifty- and sixty-hour weeks and try to cure it all with high doses of espresso, television, and antidepressants. Any hope of having true, lasting peace in the midst of this is, for many, a pipe dream.

Still, Scripture comes to us and tells us that the fruit of the Spirit is peace. What can that mean for us in a world like ours?

The Hebrew word for "peace" is *shalom*. It means more than just the absence of conflict. It is a positive state of inner harmony and well-being. This kind of peace consists of three attitudes: (1) self-acceptance; (2) positive hope for the world; and (3) confidence in one's future. Self-acceptance helps us to be at peace with ourselves. Guilt and feelings of inadequacy and worthlessness are not constantly waging war on our psyche; rather, we are glad to be the person God made us to be. Positive hope for the world helps keep us from the constant turmoil of wondering what horrible news the headlines will bring next. We know who holds the future! And confidence about one's future means we don't have to fret and stew over whether we will ever "make something of ourselves." We know the real issue is what *God* will make of us, and God never fails. Knowing that is real peace!

This lesson will help you to discover what peace is and how you can have it more consistently in your own life.

Start It *(15 minutes)*

A Moment of Silence

Observe two minutes of silence to start your meeting. Have someone in the group keep track of the time. Be sure to turn off cell phones. Relax and close your eyes. Rather than thinking about all you should be doing, repeat a Scripture in your mind over and over. Two good ones to use are "Be still, and know that I am God" (Psalm 46:10a) or "Thou wilt keep him in perfect peace, whose mind is stayed on thee: because he trusteth in thee" (Isaiah 26:3, KJV).

After the two minutes are up, choose one or two of the following questions to answer and share with the group:

- **Were you able to experience peace during the two minutes of silence? Explain.**

- **What natural setting comes to mind for you when you hear the word *peace*? What makes this place seem so peaceful to you?**

- **At what point in your life do you remember feeling most at peace? What helped you feel that way?**

- **What destroys your peace? What encourages your peace?**

Study It *(45-60 minutes)*

> If you have a large group, form smaller groups of four to seven people to answer the discussion questions. At the end of the Study It section, allow time for the subgroups to report to the whole group.

1. How would you define the kind of peace Paul is talking about in Galatians 5:22? Mention both what you think it includes and what you think it doesn't include.

Read the quotation from Harry Emerson Fosdick.

2. Notice the date of the quotation. Consider the horrors and the stresses of the age Fosdick was living in. How do those stresses compare with today's stresses?

"Here in this immediate, factual world we see such catastrophe and brutality as will make our generation rememberable for its horror many a century from now. And yet we inhabit as well a spiritual world, with intellectual insights, with ideals of beauty and loveliness, with faiths and friendships, and with aspirations that lay hold on God and goodness. If we could only live all in one world or all in the other, we might have peace, but what tension is involved in having to live in both!"

Harry Emerson Fosdick, *Living Under Tension*, 1941

3. Do you experience the tension Fosdick describes when he writes of living both in the world and in the kingdom of God? How does that tension affect our sense of peace? How can we have peace in these times?

4. Choose at least one of the following passages. Read and discuss the verses. What promise does the passage hold for our world? How would it affect a person's sense of peace if they truly believed this promise?

  • Isaiah 9:2-7
  • Isaiah 11:6-9
  • Isaiah 32:17-20
  • Micah 4:2-4
  • Revelation 21:1-4

Read Luke 2:14 and Ephesians 2:14-18.

5. How has God provided peace for us? Describe the peace that comes from God.

6. People worldwide long for peace between nations and a sense of personal, internal peace. Why do you think people long so for peace? Why do you think peace is so elusive in our world?

7. In what ways is one's personal peace dependent on or independent of external surroundings?

Read 1 Peter 3:8-12.

8. How can we seek peace and pursue it?

9. What's the connection between peace and unity? What's the difference between true peace and "peace at any cost"?

Read James 3:13–18.

10. Describe what a wise and peaceful person's life is like. Contrast that with what a "worldly-wise" person is like.

11. How does the Holy Spirit grow the fruit of peace in our lives? What is our role in that process? You may want to look at Philippians 4:6-7.

Close It *(15-30 minutes)*

Review the options in the Live It section of this session and make plans as a group to complete one of these activities prior to moving on to the next session. This is your opportunity to move from theory to practice—*carpe diem!*

Pray It

Share prayer requests and close in prayer. Be sure to ask God to guide your efforts as you plan and carry out a Live It activity.

Plan It

What activity are we going to do?

When are we doing this?

Where will this take place?

Other: special instructions/my responsibility

Option 1

Individually, do the exercise at the beginning of the session (page 34) each day for a week. A good time to do this is in the morning, to set the tone for your day. However, doing it in the evening can be a good way to unwind; and better still would be to do it in both the morning and the evening!

Find a place to get away for a few minutes. Turn off any radios or televisions that are within hearing distance. Relax and remember to focus on repeating a Scripture in your mind over and over. Again, two good ones to use are "Be still, and know that I am God" (Psalm 46:10a); or "Thou wilt keep him in perfect peace, whose mind is stayed on thee: because he trusteth in thee" (Isaiah 26:3, KJV). Do this for two to three minutes. You may want to use this exercise to begin a time of prayer.

Meet with your group at the end of the week and talk about how you grew in peace this week.

Option 2

As a group, take a one-hour silent retreat. Go to a park, a church member's farm, or another natural setting. Do not talk for one hour. In silence, explore the setting. What does what you see say to you about God and God's provision of peace? Focus on what you are seeing and experiencing, and not on stewing over your week. Examine all the layers of the life around you, from the tallest trees down to what is crawling in the grass and living on the leaves of the trees and bushes. After the hour is over, gather the group and talk about your insights into God's peace.

Option 3

Some churches have responded to what the Bible says about peace and loving your enemy by adopting official statements of pacifism. These churches are known as "peace churches" and include groups such as the Amish, the Mennonites, the Church of the Brethren, and the Friends (or Quakers).

Find a peace church in your area and invite their pastor to speak to your group about why they embrace pacifism. You may even want to attend a worship service at their church. Find out what their church does to support peace efforts around the world. For example, many peace churches support an organization called Christian Peacemaker Teams.

Visit the Christian Peacemaker Teams Web site (www.cpt.org) and discuss whether your group should become involved in this group's activities or in any kind of worldwide peacemaking efforts. Follow through on any decisions you make.

Option 4

In your group, read the prayer of St. Francis of Assisi aloud, pausing briefly after each line:

Lord, make me an instrument of your peace.
Where there is hatred, let me sow love;
where there is injury, pardon;
where there is doubt, faith;
where there is despair, hope;
where there is darkness, light;
and where there is sadness, joy.
O Divine Master, grant that I may not so much seek
to be consoled as to console;
to be understood as to understand;
to be loved as to love.
For it is in giving that we receive;
it is in pardoning that we are pardoned;
and it is in dying that we are born to eternal life.

Discuss how the entire prayer describes how one can be an instrument of God's peace. Then choose one day this week when your group can practice being instruments of God's peace. Purposefully look for the situations mentioned in the prayer (hatred, injury, doubt, despair, darkness, sadness). Seek to bring love, pardon, faith, hope, light, and joy into those situations. You may also want to memorize this prayer. Then, get together and discuss both the actions the group took to be instruments of God's peace and how your awareness of situations that benefit from God's peace increased.

Option 5

To each person in your group, assign one of the six populated continents (North America, South America, Australia, Africa, Asia, and Europe) or the Middle East. Give everyone a few days to research his or her assigned area to learn about political and social unrest in that area.

Then come together and have each person give a brief report on what they learned. Gather around a globe. Systematically pray "around the world," allowing each person to touch each region on the globe and pray that God's peace will overcome whatever unrest or violence is present there. Also pray that God's children will be sent around the globe to work as agents and ambassadors of God's peace.

You may find that after this activity, members of your group feel called to become involved in God's work around the world. Pray together and encourage each other to enthusiastically answer God's call.

Debrief It

After experiencing this session's Live It activity, discuss these questions as a group:

- **On a scale of 1 (low) to 10 (high), how would you rank this experience for yourself? Why?**

- **What was the most important insight you gained from this experience?**

- **How can you incorporate this quality into your life regularly?**

Journal It

The following space is provided for you to record your personal thoughts, reflections, impressions, or feelings about this session's topic and Live It activity.

Patience

Of all the qualities of the fruit of the Spirit listed in Galatians 5:22-23, patience may be the most difficult to acquire. In this world of instant gratification and high-speed Internet, who has time to deal with waiting, persevering, enduring, or long-suffering? We are too busy. Our finances are stretched too thin. Our kids are in trouble. We are more likely to demand, "Lord, give me patience and I want it now!" than to practice patience by simply waiting on God to work through our circumstances.

Patience *is* waiting. But it is also hoping, trusting, having faith, and being content with the knowledge that we don't have to be in control. Patience does not come naturally to us; it is a fruit of a life directed by the Spirit. We become patient when we practice patience by relinquishing our plans to God and waiting on him.

This lesson will help you learn more about how to practice and develop patience in your life.

**The Reward of
a Patient Gardener**

It's one of the world's rarest flowers—so rare, that it was seen in bloom only about twenty times in the United States in the last century. Its scarcity isn't the only thing that has made as many as 76,000 people line up for a look at it.

The *titan arum* is also the world's largest bloom. Just the bloom can measure eight feet tall and four feet across. The plant, which is native to Indonesia, must be tended patiently and exactingly for weeks or months before the grower is rewarded with a bloom. The plant blooms only a few times in its forty-year life span and the bloom only lasts about seventy-two hours before it collapses on itself due to its tremendous weight.

But what makes this rare flower worth the wait isn't its size either, but rather its scent. *Scent* may be too polite a word. The flower is also known as the corpse flower. Its scent has been described as a nauseating, rotten-flesh, or ripe manure smell. In fact, in one nursery in Michigan, the plant had to be moved outside when it was in full bloom, and even so, people reported that the smell "would take your breath away" if you were twenty yards downwind of it.

Start It *(15 minutes)*

The Patient Gardener

Have someone read aloud the story in the margin. Then discuss these questions:

- **What makes the story of the corpse flower a story about patience?**

- **Is this flower worth the wait? Why and why not?**

- **What parallels can you make from this story to times in your life when you've had to be patient?**

Study It *(45-60 minutes)*

> If you have a large group, form smaller groups of four to seven people to answer the discussion questions. At the end of the Study It section, allow time for the subgroups to report to the whole group.

Read the margin note on page 49.

1. How do these words affect your understanding of what the word *patience* means? What does it mean to be patient?

2. What situations in life call for patience? What makes being patient challenging?

> The thesaurus lists the following words under the entry for *patience*: Tolerance, acceptance, leniency, sweet reasonableness, forbearance, sufferance, endurance, long-suffering, stoicism, fortitude, perseverance, uncomplainingness, nonresistance.
>
> **Taken from *Roget's International Thesaurus, Fourth Edition***

Read the following examples of impatience:

- *Exodus 24:12-18; 32:1-4*
- *Habakkuk 1:1-4*
- *Luke 10:38-42*

3. What makes people impatient? Is impatience always wrong?

4. What does our impatience say about our character? about our attitude toward others?

5. When has your own impatience caused you trouble?

6. Look up the following passages and quickly jot down what you learn about patience. You may want to divide these references among the group members. Discuss your insights with the entire group.

- *Proverbs 14:29*
- *Proverbs 15:18*
- *Proverbs 19:11*
- *Proverbs 25:15*

- *Romans 12:12*
- *1 Corinthians 13:4*
- *Ephesians 4:2*
- *2 Timothy 4:2*

7. Why is patience a particularly important virtue for Christians? How should we exhibit patience in our lives?

8. What good does being patient bring about?

9. How would your life be different if you exhibited more patience? How would having more patience affect your walk with God? your relationships with others?

10. How does the Holy Spirit grow patience in our lives? What is our role in that process?

Close It (15-30 minutes)

Review the options in the Live It section of this session and make plans as a group to complete one of these activities prior to moving on to the next session. This is your opportunity to move from theory to practice—*carpe diem!*

Pray It

Share prayer requests and close in prayer. Be sure to ask God to guide your efforts as you plan and carry out a Live It activity.

Plan It

What activity are we going to do?

When are we doing this?

Where will this take place?

Other: special instructions/my responsibility

Part 2: live it

Option 1

Practice patience for yourself and patience for others by learning to juggle together. Plan for a half-hour practice session. Everyone will need two to three lightweight scarves.

Here are the instructions. Have everyone stand in a circle holding one scarf in their dominant hand. The first motion to practice is tossing the scarf up diagonally across your body. Then with the opposite hand, catch the scarf with a downward motion. Once you've mastered the toss up, catch down motion, practice with two scarves.

Hold one scarf in each hand. Toss the first one as before, and toss the second one before catching the first one. The rhythm is toss, toss, catch, catch. Some people say, "Criss, cross, applesauce," as a reminder to toss the scarves diagonally.

Practice this for several minutes. As some in the group get the hang of it, have them offer help to those still working on it.

If you'd like to try three scarves, here's what to do. Hold two scarves in one hand and one scarf in the other. Toss one of the two scarves, toss the one scarf in the opposite hand before catching the first scarf. Toss the third scarf before catching the second scarf. It sounds complicated, but with patience and practice, you're sure to get it!

After practicing for a half-hour or so, stop and talk about the patience required to learn a new skill.

Option 2

As a group, practice patience by volunteering to teach a class of toddlers or preschoolers during a worship service this week. If that's not possible, group members may want to spend a morning or an afternoon as helpers in their childrens' classrooms.

Option 3

As individuals, choose one day this week and spend it in perfect patience. Discuss in advance with the group what it will mean to spend a day in perfect patience. In addition to your regular activities, do at least one or two of these patience-stealers:

• Go to the grocery store at 5 p.m.
• Run errands during rush hour.
• Go to the bank during the lunch hour.
• Visit your city's rec center for a workout in the afternoon after school lets out.
• Drive past a school just as parents are dropping off or picking up children.
• Prepare a meal with children.
• Take care of business that requires you to call an automated customer service number.

During the day, keep a mental list of annoyances and your responses to them. How difficult was it to respond patiently in each situation? Get together with the group and discuss your patience successes and failures. Consider how patience helped you.

Option 4

Choose an evening to get together as a group and simply sit in silent reflection. Plan on about an hour of silence. It will be important both to start this activity on time and to end it on time. During the silence, individuals may choose to pray, to meditate, or to reflect on their day or their life's goals, but individuals may not read, speak, write, or listen to music. At the end of the hour, discuss your level of patience during this activity. Were you peaceful or restless? Was the hour positive or negative? Were you anxious about the presence of others in the room? Were you anxious about spending an hour without being outwardly productive? Were you able to enjoy time with God or did thoughts and impatience crowd their way in? What insights did you have into your own character—is your life characterized by patience?

Option 5

Practice patience by going on an all-day outing with everyone in the group, and bring the children along if you have them. You may choose to go hiking or to a zoo or museum. Plan how you will handle meals, transportation, fees, and the gathering of any needed equipment or supplies. As much as possible, stay together during the entire day. Have group members pay special attention to times during the day when patience is required or stretched.

Debrief It

After experiencing this session's Live It activity, discuss these questions as a group:

- **On a scale of 1 (low) to 10 (high), how would you rank this experience for yourself? Why?**

- **What was the most important insight you gained from this experience?**

- **How can you incorporate this quality into your life regularly?**

Journal It

The following space is provided for you to record your personal thoughts, reflections, impressions, or feelings about this session's topic and Live It activity.

Kindness

The Greek word translated as *kindness* in Galatians 5:22 is *chrestotes* (khray-stot'-ace). It means "goodness of heart," and carries with it the idea of serviceableness, graciousness, and kindness.

Those are all virtues that are desperately needed yet sadly lacking in our world. We do not live in a society that practices kindness and graciousness to others as a rule. Oh sure, we give gifts to others, we follow rules of etiquette, we say please and thank you. But how often are our gestures true kindness rather than just the obligations of polite society?

Scripture tells us that true kindness is treating the other person as a more important person than we consider ourselves to be. It's offering cold water to those parched with thirst. It's providing true justice to those who are oppressed. It's turning the other cheek. It's giving someone our tunic when they've already taken our cloak.

When we live by the Holy Spirit, he grows kindness in us. The Holy Spirit changes us from the inside out so that we become aware and sensitive to the needs of others around us, until we feel an overwhelming, loving compulsion to reach out in active kindness to others.

This lesson will help you explore the role and power of kindness in our world. It will help you consider how you will grow in kindness as the Holy Spirit works in and through you.

Start It *(15 minutes)*

A Kind Touch

Stand up and form a circle. Have everyone turn to the right and massage the shoulders of the person in front of him or her. After thirty seconds, participants turn around and repeat the process for the person now in front of them. See if you can feel any of the tension relax in your own shoulders and in the person you are massaging. Appropriate touching can be an act of kindness.

After sitting down, briefly discuss these questions.

- **How does a kind touch make you feel? encouraged? supported? worthwhile? loved?**

- **What other "touches" can be considered acts of kindness? Can even a handshake be an act of kindness? Why?**

- **Why is simple kindness so powerful?**

Study It *(45-60 minutes)*

> If you have a large group, form smaller groups of four to seven people to answer the discussion questions. At the end of the Study It section, allow time for the subgroups to report to the whole group.

1. Describe kindness by telling a story about a kind person you know. What are kind people like? What do kind people do?

Read Galatians 5:22-25.

2. Kindness may seem like a "weaker" virtue than love, which is mentioned first in the list of the fruit of the Spirit. Why do you think both kindness and love are included?

3. Why is kindness perceived as such an important virtue to Christians and non-Christians both?

Read Jeremiah 9:24; Jeremiah 31:3; Hosea 11:4; and Romans 2:4.

4. In what ways does God practice kindness? Why is it important that God is kind?

Read the quotation from the essay "Simply Complicated."

5. How do people miss seeing God's kind nature? What can Christians do to help the world see the kindness of God?

6. Read the following passages on kindness. You may want to divide them among the group members. Jot down your insights and share them with the group.

- *Proverbs 11:17*
- *Proverbs 12:25*
- *Proverbs 14:31*
- *Luke 6:27-35*
- *1 Corinthians 13:4*
- *Ephesians 4:32*
- *1 Thessalonians 5:15*
- *2 Timothy 2:22-24*
- *2 Peter 1:5-9*

Read the information in the margin that's taken from The Random Acts of Kindness Foundation.

7. What motivates people in general to be kind? What difference does kindness make in the world?

8. What should motivate Christians to be kind? Should there be a different goal when Christians (rather than non-Christians) show kindness to others?

9. What happens when we are kind to Christians? to non-Christians?

"As people tap into their own generous human spirit and share kindness with one another, they discover for themselves the power of kindness to effect positive change. When kindness is expressed, healthy relationships are created, community connections are nourished, and people are inspired to pass kindness on."

From the Random Acts of Kindness Foundation Web site

www.actsofkindness.org

10. How does the Holy Spirit grow kindness in us? What is our role in that process?

Close It *(15-30 minutes)*

Review the options in the Live It section of this session and make plans as a group to complete one of these activities prior to moving on to the next session. This is your opportunity to move from theory to practice—*carpe diem!*

Pray It

Share prayer requests and close in prayer. Be sure to ask God to guide your efforts as you plan and carry out a Live It activity.

Plan It

What activity are we going to do?

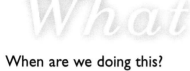

When are we doing this?

When are we doing this?

Where will this take place?

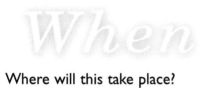

Other: special instructions/my responsibility

Option 1

Put every group member's name in a container and draw names. Make sure that no one draws the name of someone he or she lives with. You may want to consider having women draw women's names and men draw men's names. Have everyone do one act of kindness each day for the person whose name he or she drew. It could be something as simple as promising to pray daily for the person, or something that requires a sacrificial giving of time or resources.

Option 2

Show kindness to people facing serious illnesses. Ask permission to provide flowers for the people at your area's hospice facility or the oncology ward of your local hospital. Buy small bouquets of flowers and attach a note to each bouquet that expresses God's love, kindness, and hope. Deliver the bouquets as a group, with one or two people approaching each patient. Stay for just a moment with each patient, expressing your desire to brighten the patient's room and to offer a small token of kindness. Offer to pray with the patient. Afterward, get together with your group to discuss how the gifts of kindness were received.

Option 3

Buy passes to your town's budget movie theater or buy coupons for small ice cream cones at a local ice cream shop. Attach a note to each pass or coupon that says something like, "This act of kindness is provided by the people at First Church." You may want to list your church's address and service times, too. Then head to a popular shopping area in your town and hand out the passes. Be sure to offer friendly smiles and to be gently polite. If anyone asks why you're doing this, just say, "We wanted to show kindness to our community." If people decline the offer, just smile and offer the pass or coupon to someone else. After you've handed out the passes, get together and talk about what it was like to offer kindness to the community.

Option 4

Identify a family in your church or Christian fellowship that you can bombard with kindness. Discuss how to do that. You don't necessarily need to choose a needy family—anyone can benefit from a week of kindness. Maybe your pastor's family would like to know you appreciate them. Or perhaps the family of a new Christian needs to see kindness in action. Draw up a plan for showing kindness to that family. Perhaps you could send the family a gift basket for an evening of entertainment. Include gift certificates to a fun restaurant as well as tickets to a local movie, show, or event. You may also want to include a home-baked dessert, as well as a card with kind and encouraging words from each member of your group.

Option 5

Have each member of the group show kindness by talking to a visitor at your church's next worship service. The members of your group may want to invite those people out for a meal after the service. Make it a point to show deep Christian love and kindness as you make friends and get to know this visitor. Then, meet with the group and discuss how it went. What happened when you showed kindness and friendship to a stranger?

Debrief It

After experiencing this session's Live It activity, discuss these questions as a group:

- **On a scale of 1 (low) to 10 (high), how would you rank this experience for yourself? Why?**

- **What was the most important insight you gained from this experience?**

- **How can you incorporate this quality into your life regularly?**

Journal It

The following space is provided for you to record your personal thoughts, reflections, impressions, or feelings about this session's topic and Live It activity.

Goodness

"Good" is not as good as it used to be. For those who wish to excel, if their work is marked "good," they may feel a bit disappointed. On most scales these days, "good" is at most a second-notch rating. There is usually one above it, a possible rating of "excellent" or "superior," or at least "very good."

So when we hear that one aspect of the fruit of the Spirit is goodness, we may not fully appreciate its value. What we have to understand is that this was written in a time when *goodness* really meant something. When the world was created in all its beauty, God could make no higher evaluation of it than that it was "good." When Jesus was called "good," he took pains to point out that it was too high an evaluation, for "no one is good—except God alone" (Mark 10:18). Whoa! That changes the situation entirely!

We are called as Christians to manifest the fruit of goodness, and yet once we fully understand the strength of that word, we find that no one is good except God alone! It is at this point in our dilemma that we must understand that goodness can only be displayed by someone who has God within him or her.

This lesson will help you to see what it means to be good by having God within you. Through what you read and hear from others, as well as through what you do individually and with others, you'll learn that reaching the standard of "good" is not so bad after all.

Start It *(15 minutes)*

A Good Definition

To get started with today's lesson, choose one or two of the following questions to answer with your group:

- **What slang words are used for the word *good* today? How many can you list?**

- **What slang words did you use as a teenager when you wanted to say something was good?**

- **If you could point to just one person you knew as a child who exemplified the meaning of the word *good*, who would it be? What about them made them seem good to you?**

Study It *(45 minutes)*

> "*Goodness* is 'benevolence'...or 'generosity'...It involves more than moral freedom from evil, but is positive and aggressive, as the Christian seeks to be good-for-something. It is being a light in darkness, food for the hungry, water for the thirsty, as one lets the light of Christ shine through him."
>
> **Herschel H. Hobbs,** *Galatians*

If you have a large group, form smaller groups of four to seven people to answer the discussion questions. At the end of the Study It section, allow time for the subgroups to report to the whole group.

Read the quotation from Herschel Hobbs.

1. How would you define *goodness*? Why is goodness important? Why does God want to grow goodness in us?

2. If you are to be truly good, why is it not enough just to avoid evil?

3. What does it mean to be aggressively good?

4. Look up each of the following Scriptures and note what it teaches about goodness. You may want to divide the passages among group members. Share your insights with the group.

- *Matthew 7:16-20*
- *Luke 6:45*
- *Luke 11:34*
- *1 Corinthians 10:24*
- *1 Corinthians 15:33*
- *Galatians 6:9-10*

- *Ephesians 2:8-10*
- *Colossians 1:9-10*
- *2 Timothy 3:16-17*
- *James 3:13*
- *James 4:17*

5. What's the difference between having the fruit of goodness and doing good? Why is it important to distinguish between the two?

learn it
live it

Read Matthew 5:13-16 and 1 Peter 2:9-12.

6. When we exhibit goodness, what are the results? for ourselves? for others? for the church? for the world?

"One of the strangest things that people say is 'I'm a good person.' I am always amazed when people claim to know that about themselves. To say, 'I try to be a good person,' on the other hand, makes perfect sense to me...Like a child pulling the covers up to keep at bay the monsters under the bed, we hide behind the mask of self and say, 'I'm a good person.' "

Kathleen Norris, *Amazing Grace: A Vocabulary of Faith*

Read the quote from Kathleen Norris.

7. What misconceptions do people have about the rewards good people receive? What "monsters" do people try to keep at bay by telling themselves they are good?

8. As Christians, why should we want to be good? As Christians, where does our goodness come from?

Read Hebrews 10:24.

9. How can you encourage each other toward goodness? Be specific.

10. How does the Holy Spirit grow goodness in our lives? What is our role in that process?

Close It *(30 minutes)*

Review the options in the Live It section of this session and make plans as a group to complete one of these activities prior to moving on to the next session. This is your opportunity to move from theory to practice—*carpe diem!*

Pray It

Share prayer requests and close in prayer. Be sure to ask God to guide your efforts as you plan and carry out a Live It activity.

Plan It

What activity are we going to do?

When are we doing this?

Where will this take place?

Other: special instructions/my responsibility

Part 2: live it

Option 1

Plan a day to clean up a local park or natural area, a schoolyard, or a litter-ridden vacant lot. If you need help picking a spot, call your city's parks and recreation department and get their recommendation for a park or recreation area that could benefit from your efforts. Prepare by making sure everyone has gloves and plenty of trash bags. You may want to bring rakes. You may also want to arrange to have a pickup available to haul away the trash you collect.

Option 2

Plan a ministry project together where you make a positive difference in your church, community, or world. This could be anything from taking a day to pass out sandwiches to the homeless, to doing some repairs on the home of a church shut-in, to collecting supplies for a foreign mission station.

First, agree on the project that you'll do this week, and pick the time. Make a list of supplies you'll need to gather or phone calls you'll need to make. Divide the tasks among the group, making sure that everyone participates. Then carry out your plans, being sure to ask God to guide and bless your efforts for his kingdom.

Option 3

Short-term service projects are great, but serving the same organization for several weeks or months will give you a different perspective into what it means to be an agent of goodness in the world. Adopt a local helping organization that your group can assist on a long-term basis. For example, your group may choose to volunteer as tutors/mentors for your local Boys and Girls Club for a semester, or you may choose to be volunteers at a nursing home for several weeks or months.

Option 4

It has been said that "all it takes for evil to succeed is for good people to do nothing." In light of that, plan a project where your group works to counter some evil you see in your neighborhood or in the world. Perhaps it is having a letter writing campaign on a local issue of concern to your group, such as the plight of the homeless in your town; on a political issue, such as limiting pornography on the Internet; or for an international organization, such as Amnesty International, the Salvation Army, or Compassion International.

With some controversial issues, you may want to have a time of discussing it as a class before making a decision, in order to get a sense of how everyone feels about it. Sometimes agreement is assumed where there is in fact no agreement. Don't act unless your group agrees strongly about the chosen issue.

Option 5

Have each group member work on a personal behavioral issue where, like Paul in the book of Romans, you have had difficulty being good. Have each person start by reading Romans 7:18-25. Then pray and meditate on why you have struggled in this area of your life. Ask for Christ's presence and strength in changing this behavior. If there is a person you trust, confide in him or her about your struggle, tell him or her your goals for change, and then have the person hold you accountable. This could be done by reporting to your accountability partner on your progress each week. When sharing about this experience with the group, people need not specify the nature of the behavioral issue, but only what they did to address it and how much success they felt they had in changing.

Debrief It

After experiencing this session's Live It activity, discuss these questions as a group:

- **On a scale of 1 (low) to 10 (high), how would you rank this experience for yourself? Why?**

- **What was the most important insight you gained from this experience?**

- **How can you incorporate this quality into your life regularly?**

Journal It

The following space is provided for you to record your personal thoughts, reflections, impressions, or feelings about this session's topic and Live It activity.

Faithfulness

Faithfulness is a quality we greatly admire in others, whether it describes a spouse, a friend, or even a pet. However, it seems that in our world faith*less*ness is more common than faith*ful*ness. Spouses become disenchanted and leave. Friends stop calling and move into other circles of acquaintance. When a loved one or a friend shows himself or herself to be faithless, we feel wounded and disillusioned. One might wonder what God, the most faithful of all, thinks and feels when we are less than faithful to him.

Understanding what faithfulness is is easier than being a faithful person. To be faithful is to be constant, trustworthy, and reliable. In another sense, to be faithful is to be devoted. In yet another sense, to be faithful is simply to be *full* of faith, or to *keep* faith in someone or something. It is fitting that we would grow in faithfulness as the Holy Spirit grows his fruit in us. As we grow spiritually, we cannot help but grow more faithful toward the object of our faith—our gracious heavenly Father!

This lesson will help you consider your own faithfulness toward God. You'll explore biblical exhortations to be full of faith, and you'll also be challenged to let the Holy Spirit help you grow an abundant crop of faithfulness.

Start It *(15 minutes)*

Faithfully Reliable?

Review the following list of people, institutions, and things that we rely on all the time. Consider which ones you rely on most, and rank them in order of importance to you.

_____ the news media

_____ your physician

_____ your bank

_____ your vehicle

_____ the Food and Drug Administration

_____ your family

_____ your best friend

_____ your boss

_____ your pastor

_____ the government

Compare everyone's lists and talk about why you ranked the list the way you did. Then discuss these questions:

- **Why does it matter whether these people and things are faithful?**

- **Why is faithfulness important?**

Study It *(45-60 minutes)*

> If you have a large group, form smaller groups of four to seven people to answer the discussion questions. At the end of the Study It section, allow time for the subgroups to report to the whole group.

1. What's the difference between having faith and being faithful? What's the connection between the two?

Read the quote from Charlie Peacock.

2. How does what Peacock says epitomize what it means to be faithful?

Read Isaiah 24:5; Jeremiah 11:10; and Matthew 24:3-14.

3. What is faithfulness? In what ways is a Christian to be faithful?

"I've decided my work is to tell the truth, to live a life framed and filled with God-thoughts about reality— what life really is. My goal is not to be a born-again Christian, a good Christian, a religious fanatic, a do-gooder, a spiritual person, a nice guy, or an American evangelical. No, I want to be an honest-to-God follower/student of Jesus..."

Charlie Peacock, *City on a Hill*

Read the statistics in the box below.

4. Would you say that American Christians are faithful followers of Christ? What indicates whether a person is faithful to God? Are those indices reliable?

Percentage of adults who attended a church service in the last seven days:		Percentage of adults who strongly agree that their religious faith is very important in their lives today:	
All adults	43%	All adults	66%
Catholics	46%	Catholics	66%
Protestants	53%	Protestants	78%
Evangelicals	86%	Evangelicals	100%
Non-evangelical born again	57%	Non-evangelical born again	87%
Non-born again	31%	Non-born again	51%
Percentage of adults who read the Bible during the week, other than at church:		**Percentage of adults who say they are Christian and are "absolutely committed" to Christianity:**	
All adults	42%	All Adults	50%
Catholics	27%	Catholic	41%
Protestants	55%	Protestant	53%
Evangelicals	88%	Evangelicals	86%
Non-evangelical born again	61%	Non-evangelical born again	63%
Non-born again	27%	Non-born again	35%

State of the Church 2002, George Barna

5. Can you be just a little bit faithful? Why or why not? What is the process of growing in faithfulness or becoming faithful?

Read Matthew 25:14-30.

6. What made the first two servants faithful? What happened to them?

7. What made the last servant unfaithful? What happened to him?

8. What does our faithfulness or unfaithfulness say about our attitude toward our master?

9. Can a person be faithful for the wrong reasons? What should motivate a Christian to be faithful to God?

Read 2 Timothy 2:3-6.

10. This passage mentions a good soldier, a victorious athlete, and a hardworking farmer. What characteristics do these three have in common? What role does faithfulness play in each one's success?

Read 2 Timothy 4:6-8.

11. What does it mean to keep the faith? How was Paul faithful? What lessons from Paul's life can you apply to your own life?

Close It *(15-30 minutes)*

Review the options in the Live It section of this session and make plans as a group to complete one of these activities prior to moving on to the next session. This is your opportunity to move from theory to practice—*carpe diem!*

Pray It

Share prayer requests and close in prayer. Be sure to ask God to guide your efforts as you plan and carry out a Live It activity.

Plan It

What activity are we going to do?

When are we doing this?

Where will this take place?

Other: special instructions/my responsibility

Part 2: live it

Option 1

Spend time as a group brainstorming ways to complete the sentence, "A faithful Christian…" Think of what a Christian does, what a Christian thinks, and what a Christian is. Then, as individuals, pay attention to your own life for one full day. In what ways were you faithful? In what ways did you fall short of faithfulness? Take note of each time you were tempted to be disloyal or false. Then get back together and discuss what you learned.

Option 2

Do the brainstorming activity described in Option 1. Then, have each person pick two or three things from the list that he or she would like to do more faithfully. Have each person get with a partner and discuss what he or she would like to do to be a more faithful person. Have pairs act as accountability partners this week. Each can telephone the other and pray for the other to support the partner's efforts to live a more faithful life.

Option 3

Have those in your group who are married recall the vows they each made to their spouse on their wedding day. Can anyone remember specifically what they promised? Did anyone worry about whether they'd be able to live by their vows? Consider as a group what vows you each might make to God. Does the idea of making vows of fidelity to God frighten or concern you? Have each person write a vow of fidelity to God at the top of a large sheet of paper—you may want to purchase blank certificates from a stationery store for this.

Then have a faithfulness ceremony. Have each person stand and recite his or her vow to the Lord. After each person speaks, have the rest of the group gather around him or her and pray, asking God to help that person be faithful. Then have everyone sign that person's vow as witnesses. Continue until all participants have recited their vows and been prayed for.

Option 4

Hold a Faithfulness Awards Ceremony. Draw names. Have everyone consider the faithful life of the person whose name he or she drew. Everyone should find a small token of faithfulness to give to that person. For example, someone might choose a relay runner's baton to give to his or her person because of how that person has faithfully passed on the faith to others. Give everyone a few days to plan their awards. Then meet again for the ceremony. Have each participant describe the faithful life of his or her assigned person and then present the award while everyone else applauds. After the ceremony, continue the celebration by sharing a meal or having a dessert reception. Talk about how you can all continue to live faithful lives.

Option 5

We become more faithful to God when our love for God grows. Individually, spend time loving God this week. Set aside a half-hour at the beginning of every day this week to sit quietly and simply meditate on the goodness and perfection of God. Don't pray about your worries or needs. Simply tell God why you love him and thank him for who he is. Take note during the week of how this time affects what you do during the day. How does this time of adoration affect your faithfulness to God? Discuss this activity the next time you meet together as a group.

Debrief It

After experiencing this session's Live It activity, discuss these questions as a group:

- **On a scale of 1 (low) to 10 (high), how would you rank this experience for yourself? Why?**

- **What was the most important insight you gained from this experience?**

- **How can you incorporate this quality into your life regularly?**

Journal It

The following space is provided for you to record your personal thoughts, reflections, impressions, or feelings about this session's topic and Live It activity.

Gentleness

Gentleness may seem an odd virtue to include in the fruit of the Spirit. Our culture tends to value power more than it values gentleness. But looking at the meaning of this word helps us understand this virtue. Biblical gentleness isn't passive, rather it's a deliberate attitude of courtesy, mildness, meekness, and humility. It's having a friendly and quiet spirit in dealing with others and in dealing with one's circumstances.

When some of us think of the fruit of gentleness, we despair. We look at ourselves and lament: "I am anything but gentle. It's just not in my temperament." We can see that Jesus was gentle. In Matthew 11:29, Jesus describes himself as gentle and humble in heart. We know that as Christians we are to be like Jesus. Being consistently gentle, however, seems beyond the realm of possibility. But gentleness is a quality of the fruit of the Spirit. The Holy Spirit can grow the entire fruit of the Spirit in every Christian. It has nothing to do with temperament!

In this lesson, you'll explore what the Bible means when it says to be gentle, and you'll consider how the Holy Spirit will grow gentleness in you.

Start It *(15 minutes)*

How Gentle Are They?

Together, consider each of the following people (both real and fictional) and rate them on a scale of gentleness, 1 being low and 10 being high.

Jesse Ventura	1	2	3	4	5	6	7	8	9	10
Peter Parker/Spider-Man	1	2	3	4	5	6	7	8	9	10
Gloria Steinem	1	2	3	4	5	6	7	8	9	10
Rosa Parks	1	2	3	4	5	6	7	8	9	10
Clark Kent/Superman	1	2	3	4	5	6	7	8	9	10
Jesus	1	2	3	4	5	6	7	8	9	10
Hillary Clinton	1	2	3	4	5	6	7	8	9	10
Gandhi	1	2	3	4	5	6	7	8	9	10
Martin Luther King, Jr.	1	2	3	4	5	6	7	8	9	10
Mother Teresa	1	2	3	4	5	6	7	8	9	10

Then, choose one or two of the following questions to discuss as a group:

- **Who are some gentle people that you admire? that the world admires? Are they admired for their gentleness or for some other characteristic?**

- **When has gentleness made a difference in your life?**

- **Do gentle people or powerful people make the most impact in the world? Explain.**

Study It *(45-60 minutes)*

> If you have a large group, form smaller groups of four to seven people to answer the discussion questions. At the end of the **Study It** section, allow time for the subgroups to report to the whole group.

1. Describe a time when you were treated with gentleness.

2. How do people misunderstand gentleness? What are the dangers of those misinterpretations?

Read the margin note.

3. What does it really mean to be gentle? Are there times when Christians shouldn't be gentle? Explain.

The International Standard Bible Encyclopedia says, "This gift (of gentleness) enables believers to correct an erring brother or an opponent without arrogance, anger, or impatience; it is also a dominant attitude when believers must make a defense for the hope that is within them."

4. What do the following passages teach you about gentleness? You may want to divide this list among the group members. Have everyone report their insights to the whole group.

- Proverbs 15:1
- Proverbs 25:15
- 2 Corinthians 10:1-2
- Galatians 6:1
- Philippians 4:4-8

- 1 Thessalonians 2:5-9
- 1 Timothy 3:1-5
- 2 Timothy 2:22-26
- 1 Peter 3:1-5
- 1 Peter 3:15-17

Read Psalm 93:1-4 and Isaiah 40:11.

5. Do you relate more to the idea of God being powerful or gentle? Explain. How can God be both powerful and gentle?

6. Why do you think it's important to God that his children be gentle?

7. Are Christians known by their gentleness? Why or why not? What would the ramifications be if Christians became generally known as a gentle group of people?

Read the passages listed in the margin.

8. Was Jesus always gentle? Explain.

Gentle Jesus, Meek and Mild?
• John 2:13-16
• Matthew 23:33
• Matthew 16:22-23
• Matthew 17:17
• Mark 4:39

9. How does a gentle person protest a wrong? stand up for another? change the world?

10. Review the following list of people. How can you demonstrate gentleness to them? For the sake of time, pick two or three of the list to discuss, but go back on your own and consider each one.

- yourself
- your spouse
- your children
- other people's children
- your parents
- your in-laws

- the elderly
- Christians
- Christians in other denominations
- non-Christians
- those in another political party

- those hostile to Christianity
- those whose moral code you don't agree with
- those who do you harm

11. How does the Holy Spirit grow gentleness in us? What is our role in that process?

Close It (15-30 minutes)

Review the options in the Live It section of this session and make plans as a group to complete one of these activities prior to moving on to the next session. This is your opportunity to move from theory to practice—carpe diem!

Pray It

Share prayer requests and close in prayer. Be sure to ask God to guide your efforts as you plan and carry out a Live It activity.

Plan It

What activity are we going to do?

When are we doing this?

Where will this take place?

Other: special instructions/my responsibility

Option 1

Meet together and have each person bring several copies of newspapers from your area. Scan the opinion section for letters or editorials that take a position that's opposed to Christian theology or ethics, or even to Christians themselves. Then, work together to write a response, following the advice of Proverbs 15:1, and submit it to the newspaper for publication.

Option 2

Host a parents' night out for the members of your church. Get permission to use your church's nursery facilities for the event. Contact several small groups and offer to provide child service while they attend Bible study. Plan snacks, recreation, and art activities for the children. Make it a point to treat all of the children with gentleness. Afterward, talk about how the children responded to your gentleness and what made gentleness rewarding or challenging.

Option 3

As a group, get involved in a social or political cause. You might consider teenage runaways, homeless families, or at-risk children. You might consider a controversial political issue such as schools choosing not to allow Christian groups to meet, or a business owner who wants to start a local business you think is immoral. Brainstorm how you might get involved in this issue effectively while being gentle. Choose at least one way to get involved, and then follow through.

Option 4

Individually, choose two people to treat gently for two or three days. Choose one person for whom you have tender feelings. The other person should be someone with whom you often experience tension or friction. Go out of your way to treat both people gently. Note how they respond to your efforts. Get together with the group and discuss the power of gentleness.

Option 5

Show gentleness to a group not generally known for gentleness. Write letters to the inmates in a local prison, having each member of your group write to a different person. Another idea is to visit a local jail or prison as a group. Consider how you can express the gentle love of Christ to a prisoner. Get together and talk with the rest of the group about what it's like to be gentle with ungentle people. After exchanging several letters, you may want to consider meeting the prisoners you've been writing to.

Debrief It

After experiencing this session's Live It activity, discuss these questions as a group:

- **On a scale of 1 (low) to 10 (high), how would you rank this experience for yourself? Why?**

- **What was the most important insight you gained from this experience?**

- **How can you incorporate this quality into your life regularly?**

Journal It

The following space is provided for you to record your personal thoughts, reflections, impressions, or feelings about this session's topic and Live It activity.

Self-Control

Self-control is a word we hear often in life. Indeed, our culture upholds self-control as a true virtue. Exercise regimens and diets alone reveal our society's deep yearning to harness and control the excesses of life.

Yet, let's face it. As much as we wish self-control ruled the day, each of us fights a fierce battle against any form of restraint. (Who really wants to limit the amount of chocolate they consume?) Overconsumption is a problem of epidemic proportions in our world, and self-restraint is often given over to living a self-absorbed lifestyle.

This study explores the subject of self-control, the last characteristic Paul mentions in Galatians 5:22-23. Through this lesson, you will discover that self-control, like so many of the Christian virtues, can bring joy into one's life and spiritual journey.

Start It *(15 minutes)*

Control or Out-of-Control...That Is the Question

> **Leader: Set a bowl of small candies in the middle of the room. Post a sign in front of the candy that reads, "Please take only one piece of candy."**

Consider the following list of people. Discuss the role that self-control plays in their lives.

- a person on a diet
- a recovering alcoholic
- a Christian living in today's world
- a person facing an unpleasant task with a tight deadline
- an unmarried person
- a person with a long list of chores on a warm, sunny, weekend day
- a person who wants to break a bad habit
- an athlete
- a child learning to play a musical instrument
- a person with diabetes
- a child in a candy store

Next, choose one or two of the following questions to answer and share with the group:

- **Who's the most disciplined person you know? Do you find him or her to be an inspiring example or an aggravation?**

- **If you were to live the perfect self-controlled life, what would you accomplish and what would others think about you?**

- **Are you finding it difficult to eat only one piece of candy? Why or why not?**

Study It (45-60 minutes)

If you have a large group, form smaller groups of four to seven people to answer the discussion questions. At the end of the Study It section, allow time for the subgroups to report to the whole group.

Read the quote from Leonard Sweet.

1. According to Sweet, what is the core reason underlying an absence of self-control in our lives? Would you agree that the absence of self-control is as dangerous as Sweet suggests? Why or why not?

> "Hell is getting what *you* want. Hell is doing only what works for *you*. Hell is building a self based on a foundation of one. Heaven is being the self God made you to be and the self you can't become without God and the church."
> **Leonard Sweet,**
> *SoulTsunami*

2. What challenges will a Christian without self-control face?

3. How does self-control benefit a Christian?

4. What does self-control mean to a Christian? Describe a self-controlled Christian and his or her life.

5. What motivates a Christian to live a self-controlled life? What hinders a Christian from living a self-controlled life?

> "Do we in fact enjoy too much freedom? We have freedom to harm and kill each other, to fight global wars, to despoil our planet. We are even free to defy God, to live without restraints as though the other world did not exist."
>
> **Philip Yancey,**
> *The Jesus I Never Knew*

Read the quote from Philip Yancey. Also read 1 Corinthians 10:23.

6. In what ways are Christians free? How do freedom and self-control figure into the Christian's life?

Read Matthew 4:1-11.

7. How did Jesus exhibit self-control? What lessons about Jesus' self-control can you apply to your own life?

Read 1 Corinthians 9:24-27 and Philippians 3:12–4:1.

8. What insight do these passages offer regarding self-control in the everyday life of a Christian?

Read Romans 7:14-25.

9. How is the battle Paul described present in your life?

Read Romans 8:1-10.

10. Is living by the Spirit the same thing as having self-control? Explain. How does a Christian live by the Spirit?

11. How does the Holy Spirit develop self-control in our lives? What is our role in that process?

Close It *(15-30 minutes)*

Review the options in the Live It section of this session and make plans as a group to complete one of these activities prior to moving on to the next session. This is your opportunity to move from theory to practice—*carpe diem!*

Pray It

Share prayer requests and close in prayer. Be sure to ask God to guide your efforts as you plan and carry out a Live It activity.

Since this is the last session in this study, discuss what the group would like to do next. You may want to have a party to celebrate the completion of this course.

Plan It

What activity are we going to do?

When are we doing this?

Where will this take place?

Other: special instructions/my responsibility

Part 2: live it

Option 1

Discovering self-control comes with spiritual growth. As a group, agree to individually spend fifteen to thirty minutes daily for the next six days reading through the book of Galatians, chapter by chapter. Keep a brief journal about your experience. In the journal reflect on the following:
- How easy was it to initiate this devotion time?
- What almost prevented me from doing today's devotion?
- What have I learned from today's reading in Galatians?
- How can I apply this reading to my daily life?

At the end of the week, meet and talk about the daily discipline of studying God's Word.

Option 2

Have each member of the group identify one area of his or her life where he or she lacks self-control. Have everyone write his or her area on two index cards. Next, on both index cards, have each person write two or three ideas to help him or her be more self-controlled in that area. On the other side of both cards, have everyone write out 1 Corinthians 9:25.

Instruct everyone to keep one card as a reminder to work on self-control. Have each person swap the other card with someone in the group who will provide accountability and prayer support. Encourage the accountability partners to touch base during the week, checking in on each other's progress.

Option 3

Practice self-control by attending a dinner buffet together as a group this week. Resolve to be self-controlled in both the choice of what to eat and how much to eat. As you enjoy the food together, talk about the daily effort involved in being self-controlled.

Option 4

As a part of your study into the fruit of self-control, this may be a good time to review the expectations of your group. It's easy to fall into the habit of starting later and later each week. It's also easy to fall into the habit of enjoying each other's fellowship so much that Bible study and prayer lose their priority. Spend time talking about what's important to your group. What guidelines do you want to set? Then, encourage each other to practice self-control by living up to the agreement of the group.

Option 5

Prayer is an area in which many Christians would like to be more disciplined. Discuss as a group the rewards and results of having a consistent time of prayer. Then resolve as individuals to spend at least fifteen minutes (if not thirty minutes) of each day this week praying. Set up a phone chain so that each member of the group will call another member of the group to encourage him or her to pray and to mention any prayer requests. At the end of the week, gather and discuss how regular prayer affected your spiritual life and your relationship with God.

Debrief It

After experiencing this session's Live It activity, discuss these questions as a group:

- **On a scale of 1 (low) to 10 (high), how would you rank this experience for yourself? Why?**

- **What was the most important insight you gained from this experience?**

- **How can you incorporate this quality into your life regularly?**

Journal It

The following space is provided for you to record your personal thoughts, reflections, impressions, or feelings about this session's topic and Live It activity.

Learn It, Live It: Fruit of the Spirit

Please help Group Publishing, Inc., continue to provide innovative and useful resources for ministry. Please take a moment to fill out this evaluation and mail or fax it to us. Thanks!

Group Publishing, Inc.
Attention: Product Development
P.O. Box 481
Loveland, CO 80539
Fax: (970) 292-4370

● ● ●

1. As a whole, this book has been (circle one)
   not very helpful   *very helpful*
   1   2   3   4   5   6   7   8   9   10

2. The best things about this book:

3. Ways this book could be improved:

4. Things I will change because of this book:

5. Other books I'd like to see Group publish in the future:

6. Would you be interested in field-testing future Group products and giving us your feedback? If so, please fill in the information below:

Name _____

Church Name _____

Denomination _____ Church Size _____

Church Address _____

City _____ State _____ ZIP _____

Church Phone _____

E-mail _____

Really Make a Difference—
Live What You've Learned!

It's the way Bible study should be! Adults will read and discuss the Bible, then apply it to their lives in exciting new ways. After studying a subject, participants will choose engaging projects to do as a group, reinforcing what they just learned. The studies include several project options for each lesson, from easy one-night projects to more involved ideas. The four topics in this series include:

- Fruit of the Spirit *(9 lessons)*
- Prayer *(7 lessons)*
- Spiritual Disciplines *(7 lessons)*
- Spiritual Gifts *(8 lessons)*

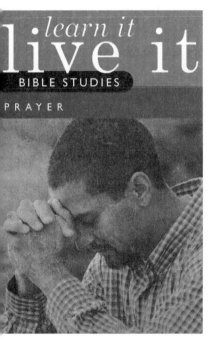

It's practical, engaging, experiential, and hands-on. Be doers and hearers of the Word!

Each kit includes one leader guide and 6 participant books:

Fruit of the Spirit
ISBN 0-7644-2556-0

Prayer
ISBN 0-7644-2557-9

Spiritual Disciplines
ISBN 0-7644-2558-7

Spiritual Gifts
ISBN 0-7644-2559-5

Look for the **Learn It, Live It Bible Studies™ Series** at your favorite Christian supplier or write:

P.O. Box 485, Loveland, CO 80539-0485.
www.grouppublishing.com

Does Your Church Offer Marriage Insurance?

Great marriages don't just happen—husbands and wives need to nurture them. They need to make their marriage relationship a priority.

That's where the newly revised HomeBuilders Couples Series® can help! The series consists of interactive 6- to 7-week small group studies that make it easy for couples to really open up with each other. The result is fun, nonthreatening interactions that build stronger Christ-centered relationships between spouses— and with other couples!

Whether you've been married for years, or are newly married, this series will help you and your spouse discover timeless principles from God's Word that you can apply to your marriage and make it the best it can be!

The HomeBuilders Couples Series Leader Guide gives you all the information and encouragement you need to start and lead a dynamic HomeBuilders small group.

The HomeBuilders Couples Series includes these life-changing studies:

Building Teamwork in Your Marriage

Building Your Marriage

Building Your Mate's Self-Esteem

Growing Together in Christ

Improving Communication in Your Marriage

Making Your Remarriage Last

Mastering Money in Your Marriage

Overcoming Stress in Your Marriage

Resolving Conflict in Your Marriage

And check out the HomeBuilders Parenting Series!

Building Character in Your Children

Establishing Effective Discipline
for Your Children

Guiding Your Teenagers

Helping Your Children Know God

Improving Your Parenting

Raising Children of Faith

Look for the **HomeBuilders Couples Series and HomeBuilders Parenting Series** at your favorite Christian supplier or write:

www.familylife.com

P.O. Box 485, Loveland, CO 80539-0485.
www.grouppublishing.com